D0761129

From Seed to Flower

By STEVEN ANDERSON

Illustrated by MARCIN PIWOWARSKI

CANTATA
LEARNING

MANKATO, MINNESOTA

WWW.CANTATALEARNING.COM

CANTATA
LEARNING

MANKATO, MINNESOTA

Published by Cantata Learning
1710 Roe Crest Drive
North Mankato, MN 56003
www.cantatalearning.com

Library of Congress Control Number: 2014956995
978-1-63290-262-7 (hardcover/CD)
978-1-63290-414-0 (paperback/CD)
978-1-63290-456-0 (paperback)

From Seed to Flower by Steven Anderson
Illustrated by Marcin Piwowarski

Book design, Tim Palin Creative
Editorial direction, Flat Sole Studio
Executive musical production and direction, Elizabeth Draper
Music arranged and produced by Steven C Music

Printed in the United States of America.

VISIT

WWW.CANTATALEARNING.COM/ACCESS-OUR-MUSIC

TO SING ALONG TO THE SONG

Every plant changes as it grows. It starts as a tiny seed. A seedling then sprouts, growing **roots** and leaves. The plant will bloom with flowers, which make seeds. Then more plants will grow. This series of changes is called a **life cycle**.

4

Now turn the page,
and sing along.

This tiny seed won't stay tiny much more.
It **germinates** when spring showers pour.

The seed starts to grow, reaching down with its roots.

A seedling sprouts leaves, and upwards it shoots.

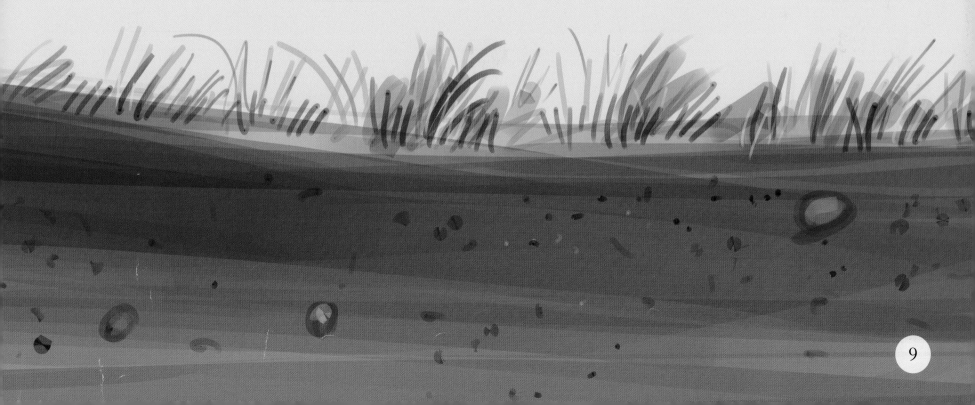

There's a cycle of life
for all living things.

Flowers begin as seeds
and then start growing
up, up, up so colorful.

The cycle's never ending.

Adult plants grow buds,
hiding colorful surprises.

They bloom into flowers
of all shapes and sizes.

12

The flowers' bright colors attract buzzing bees, bringing **pollen**, which some plants need to make seeds.

There's a cycle of life
for all living things.

Flowers begin as seeds
and then start growing
up, up, up so colorful.

The cycle's never ending.

Some seeds spread by
floating through the air.

Others are eaten by birds
or get stuck in hair.

When the seed has found a nice place on the ground,
it will sleep until spring, when rains pour down.

There's a cycle of life
for all living things.

Flowers begin as seeds
and then start growing
up, up, up so colorful.

The cycle's never ending.

21

SONG LYRICS
From Seed to Flower

This tiny seed won't stay
   tiny much more.
It germinates when
   spring showers pour.

The seed starts to grow,
   reaching down with its
roots.
A seedling sprouts leaves,
   and upwards it shoots.

There's a cycle of life
for all living things.

Flowers begin as seeds
and then start growing
up, up, up so colorful.

The cycle's never ending.

Adult plants grow buds,
hiding colorful surprises.

They bloom into flowers
of all shapes and sizes.

The flowers' bright colors
attract buzzing bees,
bringing pollen,
   which some
plants need to
   make seeds.

There's a cycle of life
for all living things.

Flowers begin as seeds
and then start growing
up, up, up so colorful.

The cycle's never ending.

Some seeds spread by
floating through the air.

Others are eaten by
   birds or
get stuck in hair.

When the seed has found
   a nice place on the
   ground,
it will sleep until spring,
   when rains pour down.

There's a cycle of life
for all living things.

Flowers begin as seeds
and then start growing
up, up, up so colorful.

The cycle's never ending.

From Seed to Flower

Rock
Steven C Music

Verse 2
Adult plants grow buds,
hiding colorful surprises.
They bloom into flowers
of all shapes and sizes.

The flowers' bright colors
attract buzzing bees,
bringing pollen, which some
plants need to make seeds.

Chorus

Verse 3
Some seeds spread by
floating through the air.
Others are eaten by birds or
get stuck in hair.

When the seed has found
a nice place on the ground,
it will sleep until spring,
when rains pour down.

Chorus (2x)

GLOSSARY

germinates—to begin to grow; rain often causes seeds to germinate.

life cycle—a series of changes that a plant goes through, from seed to flowering

pollen—small particles that plants use to make seeds

roots—the parts of a plant that grow down into the ground; roots support a plant, and they also get water and nutrients from the ground.

GUIDED READING ACTIVITIES

1. Draw a picture of a plant with a flower. Label all of the plant's parts that you know.

2. Flowers come in many different colors. What is your favorite color, and why?

3. What animals can be important in a flower's life cycle?

TO LEARN MORE

Claire Throp. *All About Flowers*. Chicago: Capstone Heinemann Library, 2015.

Lisa M. Herrington. *Seed to Plant*. New York: Children's Press, an imprint of Scholastic Inc., 2014.

Owen, Ruth. *What Do Roots, Stems, Leaves, and Flowers Do?* New York: PowerKids Press, 2015.

Sohn, Emily and Erin Ash Sullivan. *New Plants: Seeds in the Soil Patch*. Chicago: Norwood House Press, 2012.